UNITED STATES COURT OF APPEALS FOR THE EIGHTH CIRCUIT

LOCAL RULES

October 1, 2010

UNITED STATES COURT OF APPEALS
FOR THE EIGHTH CIRCUIT

CIRCUIT JUSTICE

Samuel A. Alito, Jr.. Washington, D.C.

CHIEF JUDGE

William Jay Riley... Omaha, Nebraska

CIRCUIT JUDGES

Roger L. Wollman............................ Sioux Falls, South Dakota

James B. Loken.................................. Minneapolis, Minnesota

Diana E. Murphy............................... Minneapolis, Minnesota

Kermit E. Bye... North Dakota

Michael J. Melloy...Cedar Rapids, Iowa

Lavenski R. Smith................................... Little Rock, Arkansas

Steven M. Colloton.. Des Moines, Iowa

Raymond W. Gruender...............................St. Louis, Missouri

Duane Benton.. Kansas City, Missouri

Bobby E. Shepherd................................... El Dorado, Arkansas

SENIOR CIRCUIT JUDGES

Myron H. Bright....................................... Fargo, North Dakota

John R. Gibson...................................... Kansas City, Missouri

Pasco M. Bowman.................................. Kansas City, Missouri

C. Arlen Beam.. Lincoln, Nebraska

David R. Hansen.. Cedar Rapids, Iowa

Morris S. Arnold..................................... Little Rock, Arkansas

CIRCUIT EXECUTIVE

Millie B. Adams . ...St. Louis, Missouri

CLERK

Michael E. Gans . ... St. Louis, Missouri

PREFACE

Based on Rule 47 of the Federal Rules of Appellate Procedure (FRAP), this court adopts the Eighth Circuit Rules of Appellate Procedure (8th Cir. R.), governing appeals to the court on and after September 1, 2010.

The Eighth Circuit Rules of Appellate Procedure supplement the Federal Rules of Appellate Procedure. Counsel should be familiar with both sets of rules and the federal statutes governing appeals, particularly 28 U.S.C. §§ 1291 and 1292.

For the convenience of counsel, the Eighth Circuit Rules are numbered to correspond to the Federal Rules of Appellate Procedure.

*Revised December 1, 1998
Revised April 1, 2001
Revised February 1, 2002
Revised December 1, 2002
Revised December 1, 2008
Revised December 1, 2009
Revised October 1, 2010

EIGHTH CIRCUIT RULES OF APPELLATE PROCEDURE

TABLE OF CONTENTS

TITLE I--APPLICABILITY OF RULES

Page

TITLE III-REVIEW OF A DECISION OF THE UNITED STATES TAX COURT

TITLE IV-REVIEW OR ENFORCEMENT OF AN ORDER OF AN ADMINISTRATIVE AGENCY, BOARD, COMMISSION, OR OFFICER

TITLE V-EXTRAORDINARY WRITS

TITLE VI-HABEAS CORPUS; PROCEEDINGS IN FORMA PAUPERIS

(No local rule)

TITLE VII-GENERAL PROVISIONS

RULE 3B: APPEAL INFORMATION FORM

In all civil cases except those brought under 28 U.S.C. §§ 2241, 2254, or 2255, the appellant must complete an Appeal Information Form (Form A), submit it with the notice of appeal to the clerk of the district court, and serve a copy on the appellee. The appellee may file and serve a supplemental statement (Form B) within 3 days after receiving service of Form A.   Copies of Forms A and B may be obtained from the clerk of this court or from the clerks of the district courts.

_____

Cross-References: FRAP 3, 4, 26(b);
                         FRAP Appendix, Form 1 (Notice of Appeal);
                         8th Cir. R. 33A.

_____

RULE 3C: DISMISSAL FOR FAILURE TO PROSECUTE

If an appellant fails to comply with the Federal Rules of Appellate Procedure or these rules, the clerk will notify the appellant and appellant's counsel that the appeal will be dismissed for want of prosecution unless appellant remedies the default within 14 days after the clerk issues the notice. If the appellant fails to comply within the 14-day period, the clerk will enter an order dismissing the appeal for want of prosecution and issue a certified copy of the order as the mandate to the clerk of the district court. After the appeal has been dismissed under this rule, there is no remedy for default except by order of the court. The dismissal of an appeal will not limit the court's authority to take disciplinary action against defaulting counsel in appropriate cases.

_____

Cross-Reference: FRAP 3(a)(2).

_____

RULE 10A: EXHIBITS

(a) Duty of Appellant. Subject to subparagraph (b) of 8 [th] Cir. R.10A, appellant must ensure that all trial exhibits and all relevant pre-trial exhibits, or copies thereof, are submitted to the clerk of the court appeals no later than the filing of appellant's opening brief. If the trial exhibits and the relevant pre-trial exhibits were retained by the district court, appellant must ask the clerk of the district court to forward the exhibits to the clerk of the court of appeals. If the trial exhibits and the relevant pre-trial exhibits were not retained by the district court, appellant must prepare and submit a separate appendix containing the exhibits, or copies thereof. In the event appellant fails either to ask the district court to transmit the exhibits or to prepare a separate appendix of exhibits, the appellee may take steps to ensure that all trial exhibits and all relevant pretrial exhibits, or copies thereof, are submitted to the clerk of the court of appeals no later than the filing of appellee's brief. In pro se cases, the district court will transmit the exhibits, and no separate appendix of exhibits is required. See 8 [th] Cir. R. 30A(a)(2).

(b) Physical Exhibits. Physical exhibits should not be filed with the clerk of this court unless they are referred to in the brief and examination of the exhibits would aid the court in resolving an issue raised on appeal. Counsel should contact the clerk before submitting unusually bulky or large physical exhibits. In a criminal case, evidence such as firearms and drugs may be filed only with leave of court.

RULE 11A: TRANSMISSION OF THE RECORD ON APPEAL

A certified copy of all docket entries in the proceeding below must be transmitted to the court in place of the entire record. See FRAP 11(e). The appellant's brief is due 40 days after filing of the docket entries. *See* FRAP 31(a)(1).

_____

Cross-References: FRAP 11(e), 30, 31(a);
       8th Cir. R. 30A.

_____

RULE 21A: PETITIONS FOR WRITS OF MANDAMUS AND PROHIBITION

Within 14 days after the filing of the petition, or as the court orders, the court must either dismiss the petition or direct that an answer be filed.

_____

Cross-Reference: FRAP 21.

_____

RULE 22A: DEATH PENALTY CASES

(a) Notice to the Clerk. The state attorney general or United States attorney must notify the clerk of the court promptly by telephone, fax or electronic filing when a warrant for execution is issued. The notice should provide the name of the prisoner and the time and date of the scheduled execution. Upon receipt of the notice, the clerk will contact the prisoner's counsel to determine the prisoner's plan for litigation.

(b) Emergency Nature of the Proceedings. The clerk will treat all pleadings filed after the issuance of a warrant for execution as emergency matters. Where the length or nature of the documents makes electronic filing through CM/ECF impractical, the documents must be filed with the clerk and served on opposing counsel by overnight delivery service or hand-delivery. All counsel must provide the clerk with home and other telephone numbers where they may be reached after regular business hours. The clerk will maintain business hours as may be required to facilitate the court's consideration of the proceedings.

(c) Required Information. In an application for second or successive habeas relief, the prisoner must provide the following information:

(1) the grounds for relief;

(2) a list of all pending litigation in federal or state court;

(3) the captions and case numbers of all previous habeas proceedings, including appeals to this court and certiorari petitions to the United States Supreme Court, and citations to any published state or federal court opinions;

(4) the outcome of all previous habeas petitions, including whether any prior petition was dismissed without prejudice or for failure to exhaust state remedies; and

(5) copies of all state or federal court opinions or judgments relating to the conviction and sentence if the opinions or judgments are not available electronically through PACER or Westlaw.

(d) Motions for Stay. A motion for a stay of execution should be prepared as a separate document and should be filed simultaneously with the application for second or successive habeas relief.

(e) Responses and Replies. Upon receipt of an application for a second or successive habeas or a motion for stay of execution, the clerk will contact the state attorney general or the United States attorney and set a deadline for a response to the application or motion. If counsel for the petitioner wishes to file a reply, counsel should contact the clerk and obtain a filing deadline.

(f) Other Challenges to an Execution. Within 24 hours of its filing in United States district court, the petitioner must provide the clerk with a copy of any complaint in any civil action which challenges or seeks to stay the execution. Respondent and petitioner must promptly furnish the clerk with all subsequent pleadings in the matter, and petitioner must promptly notify the clerk of any opinion or dispositive order in the matter.

Cross-Reference: FRAP 22.

RULE 22B: SECOND OR SUCCESSIVE HABEAS CORPUS AND SECTION 2255 PROCEEDINGS

(a) In any application for second or successive habeas corpus relief or for second or successive motion under 28 U.S.C. § 2255 which is filed in this court, the petitioner or movant must provide the following information:

(1) the grounds for relief;

(2) if available, the filing dates, captions, docket numbers, and courts where all prior habeas proceedings or section 2255 motions and appeals were filed; and

(3) the outcome of all former habeas proceedings or section 2255 motions and appeals, including whether any prior petition was dismissed without prejudice or for failure to exhaust state remedies.

(b) The clerk will electronically serve a copy of the application for second or successive habeas petition or section 2255 motion on the appropriate state attorney general or United States attorney.

(c) The state attorney general or United States attorney must file a response within 14 days of receipt of the application for second or successive habeas petition or section 2255 motion. The response must include:

(1) a brief response to the grounds for relief stated by petitioner or movant;

(2) information petitioner or movant has not supplied under Rule 22B(a)(2) and (3) of these local rules; and

(3) copies of orders and memorandum opinions in all former habeas

proceedings and section 2255 motions filed by petitioner or movant if the orders and opinion are not available electronically through PACER or Westlaw.

(d) Applications and responses are limited to 20 pages.

RULE 25A: ELECTRONIC (CM/ECF) AND FACSIMILE FILING; ELECTRONIC NOTICING AND SERVICE

(a) Electronic Filing. Use of the CM/ECF system is mandatory for all attorneys, unless they are granted an exemption, and is voluntary for all pro se litigants proceeding without counsel. Registration is required to obtain a password and login for use of the electronic filing system. Attorneys and pro se litigants may register to use the system through the federal courts' PACER system. The clerk will maintain training materials, as well as information about registration and system requirements on the court's website. A form to obtain an exemption is available from the court's website. Exemptions may be granted for good cause, and the clerk is authorized to determine when to grant an exemption and whether to permit a non-exempt attorney to file a document in paper format.

A filing in electronic format constitutes the official record in the appeal. Except as otherwise provided in these rules, filers should not submit paper copies of any document filed through the CM/ECF system.

Questions concerning the system, attorney registration and attorney exemptions should be directed to the clerk of court.

(b) Documents That Must Be Filed Electronically:
The following documents must be filed electronically:
* Forms A & B (8th Cir. Rule 3B);
* Appearance Forms;
* Corporate Disclosure Statements (FRAP 26.1);
* Applications to Grant or Modify Certificates of Appealability (FRAP 22b);
* Motions, Responses to Motions and Replies (FRAP 27);
* Record on Appeal Notices (FRAP 30 and 8th Cir. R. 30A);
* Status Reports Required by the Court's Orders;
* Briefs filed by CM/ECF filers (8th Cir. R. 28A)
* Addendums to briefs filed by CM/ECF filers (8th Cir. R. 28A)
* Citations of Supplemental Authorities [FRAP 28(j)];

     * Petitions for Panel Rehearing or Rehearing En Banc (FRAP 35
        and 40) and Responses as Requested by the Court;
     * Bills of Costs (FRAP 39) and Motions for Attorneys' Fees;
     * Correspondence Directed to the Clerk of the Court; and
     * Other documents as directed by the Clerk or the Court.

(c) Documents That Cannot Be Filed Electronically:
     * Documents initiating proceedings under Federal Rules of Appellate Procedure 5, 15, or 21 or petitions for review filed in the first instance in the court of appeals cannot be filed electronically and must be filed with the clerk in paper format. Only the clerk's office can initiate a new case.

     * Appendices and other record materials must be filed in paper format in accordance with the provisions of Federal Rules of Appellate Procedure 10 and 30 and Eighth Circuit Rule 30A.

     * Criminal Justice Act vouchers and attachments must be filed in paper format.

(d) Service: A Certificate of Service is required for all filings, and filers must comply with the provisions of Federal Rule of Appellate Procedure 25 and Eighth Circuit Rule 25A(a) when they file electronically. CM/ECF will generate a Notice of Docket Activity when any document is filed. This notice represents service of the document on parties who are registered participants in the CM/ECF system or who have provided the clerk with their email address. An attorney's or party's registration for electronic filing constitutes consent to service through the Notice of Docket Activity. With the exception of merits briefs as set out in 8th Cir. R. 28A(c), the filing party is not required to serve a paper or electronic copy of any electronically-filed pleading or document on any party receiving electronic notice. Filing parties must serve paper copies of pleadings or documents on parties not receiving electronic notices. In such instances, the filing party must comply with the paper service requirements of Federal Rule of Appellate Procedure 25. The filing party may determine the names and addresses of parties not participating in CM/ECF from the Notice of Docket Activity they receive when they complete a docketing transaction.

Sample Certificates of Service may be downloaded from the "Forms" Section of the court's website.

(e) Completion of the Electronic Appellate Case File: In the event the clerk receives a document in paper format, the clerk will scan the document and attach it to the public docket sheet available on PACER. The clerk will attach an electronic copy of the brief to the public docket sheet available on PACER. All documents initiating original proceedings in petitions for review or in cases under FRAP 5, 15, and 21 will be scanned and placed on the docket. Joint and Separate Appendices prepared pursuant to FRAP 30 and 8th Cir. R. 30A(b) will not be scanned and attached to the docket sheet. District court original files and transcripts and agency records used as the record on appeal will not be scanned and attached to the public docket sheet available on PACER.

(f) Filing Deadlines and Technical Requirements: Electronic filing is permitted at all times, except when the system is temporarily unavailable due to routine or emergency maintenance. An electronic filing completed at any time before midnight Central Time will be entered on the docket as of that date. The court's electronic case filing system determines the date and time a filing is completed. A filing is timely only if accomplished in accordance with deadlines set by an applicable order, rule or statute. Should technical failure prevent timely electronic filing of any document, the filing party may seek relief from the court.

All electronic versions of the pleadings must be submitted in Portable Document Format (also known as PDF or Acrobat Format). The digital version filed with the clerk must be generated by printing to PDF from the original word processing file so that the text of the digital version of the pleading may be searched and copied. However, exhibits which are submitted as attachments to an electronically-filed pleading or the Addendum may be scanned and attached if the filer does not possess a word-processing-file version of the attachment. Filers may contact the clerk's office for directions concerning the submission of scanned documents.

(g) Sealed Documents: Sealed documents must only be filed in paper format. Motions for permission to file a document under seal must also be filed in paper format. The motion should state whether the filing party believes the motion to seal may be made publically available on PACER or should remain sealed.

(h) Privacy: In compliance with the privacy policies of the Judicial Conference of the United States and in order to address the privacy concerns created by Internet access to court documents, parties must refrain from including, or must partially redact where inclusion is necessary, the following personal data identifiers from all documents filed with the court:

> 1. Minors' names (use initials only);
> 2. Social Security numbers (use last four digits only);
> 3. Dates of birth (use year of birth only);
> 4. Financial account numbers (identify the type of account and institution and

provide the last four digits of the account number); and

5. Home address information (use phrases such as the "4000 block of Elm").

6. The Addendum to a criminal brief must not include the Statement of Reasons or other confidential sentencing materials.

The filer bears sole responsibility for redacting documents.

(i) Social Security and Immigration Cases: Under the privacy policy of the Judicial Conference of the United States and various rules and statutory provisions, remote electronic public access to the CM/ECF file in appeals in Social Security cases and petitions for review in immigration cases is subject to restrictions. In order to implement these policies, the clerk will restrict remote electronic public access to documents in these cases so that only the court's judges and staff and the parties and attorneys in the case may access them electronically. No restrictions will be placed on remote electronic public access to the court's orders and opinions in Social Security and immigration cases. Any party seeking to restrict public access to orders and opinions must file a motion explaining why such relief is required. Non-parties may inspect the court's file in the case at the clerk's office.

Registered electronic filers in Social Security and immigration cases must submit their documents through CM/ECF and should comply with all of the other filing provisions of this rule. When documents are filed electronically, CM/ECF automatically locks them to restrict access to the users authorized by this order. Access to any paper document received by the clerk and scanned for entry in the CM/ECF electronic case file will be similarly restricted. Filers should note that they cannot access filings in these cases through their PACER ID and Password and must access these files through their CM/ECF Filer ID and Password.

(j) Effect of Failure to Comply with this Rule:
The clerk will contact any non-exempt attorney who submits a covered document in paper format and will bring the rule to the attorney's attention. In the event a non-exempt attorney continues to submit documents in paper format after receiving notice of the rule, the clerk is authorized to strike the filings or take other actions deemed necessary to enforce the rule.

(k) Electronic Noticing. The clerk's office will use the CM/ECF system to provide notice to all registered participants in a case. The clerk will serve a paper copy of the notice on any attorney granted an exemption and on pro se litigants not registered to use the system.

(l) Filing by Facsimile. The clerk may establish a program to permit parties to file documents by facsimile.

Rule 25B: FILING BY PRO SE LITIGANTS WHO ARE NOT REGISTERED CM/ECF FILERS

(a) General Provisions. Pro se litigants who are not registered users of the CM/ECF system may use CM/ECF to serve their pleadings on registered users of the system. When the case is docketed, the clerk will provide the pro se litigant with a listing of the parties to the case which will show whether a party can be served electronically by the clerk or must be served by mail by the pro se litigant. If a party to the appeal is a registered CM/ECF user or is represented by a registered user, the clerk will perform service on the party pursuant to the provisions of these rules, and the pro se litigant is not required to serve a paper copy of the pleading on the registered user. If a party to the appeal is not a registered user or is not represented by a registered user, the pro se litigant must serve a paper copy of the document on the party in accordance with the provisions of FRAP 25 at the same time he files the document with the clerk.

(b) Duties of the Clerk and Service on Parties to the Appeal. When a pro se litigant files a paper document with the clerk's office, the clerk will scan the document into the CM/ECF system and create a docket entry for the pleading showing its filing date. The clerk will then provide every registered user with an electronic Notice of Docket Activity. This electronic Notice of Docket Activity will constitute service of the document on the registered user for purposes of FRAP 26, and the date of the electronic Notice of Docket Activity will serve as the date of service for purposes of FRAP 26(c). Response or reply times for non-registered users who receive their service by mail will be calculated in accordance with the provisions of
FRAP 26(c).

(c) Pro Se Certificate of Service. Every document filed by a pro se litigant shall include a certificate of service which provides the date the party mailed the document to the clerk, together with the names of any parties or attorneys the pro se party served by mail. A sample pro se certificate of service can be found at Appendix B to these rules.

(d) Clerk to Provide Copy of Notice of Docket Activity. The clerk will provide the pro se filer with a paper copy of the Notice of Docket Activity showing the date the document was filed and the names of the persons the clerk served electronically.

Cross Reference: FRAP 25(a)(2)(D).

RULE 26.1A: CORPORATE DISCLOSURE STATEMENT

The Corporate Disclosure Statement must be filed within 7 days after receipt of notice that the appeal has been docketed in this court.

Cross-Reference: FRAP 26.1.

RULE 27A: ORDERS

(a) Orders the Clerk May Grant. The clerk has discretion to enter orders on behalf of the court in procedural matters including, but not limited to:

> (1) applications to file briefs exceeding the page limits set forth in these rules and the Federal Rules of Appellate Procedure;
>
> (2) extensions of time for filing briefs and records;
>
> (3) extensions of time for designating the record under 8th Cir. R. 30A(b);
>
> (4) authorization to proceed on a deferred appendix under 8th Cir. R. 30A(b)(2);
>
> (5) corrections in briefs, pleadings, or the record;
>
> (6) supplementation of the record;

(7) incorporation of records from former appeals;

(8) consolidation of appeals;

(9) substitution of parties;

(10) motions to appear as amicus curiae;

(11) requests by amicus curiae counsel to participate in oral argument by sharing time with other counsel;

(12) advancement or continuance of cases;

(13) appointment of counsel on appeal in cases prosecuted under the Criminal Justice Act;

(14) withdrawal of appearance in civil cases;

(15) extensions of time to file petitions for rehearing not to exceed 14 days;

(16) transmission of records to the Supreme Court for use in connection with petitions for writs of certiorari;

(17) entry of consent decrees in National Labor Relations Board cases and other governmental agency review cases;

(18) taxation of costs under 28 U.S.C. § 1920; and

(19) Exemptions from participation in the CM/ECF system.

If any party opposes the action requested in any of the above matters or seeks reconsideration of an order entered under this section, the clerk must submit the matter for a ruling by a judge of this court.

(b) Orders One Judge May Grant. Subject to FRAP 27(c), one judge of the court may determine any motion and exercise any power including:

(1) granting leave to appeal in forma pauperis and ordering preparation of a transcript at government expense;

(2) granting appointment of counsel for an indigent defendant proceeding under 28 U.S.C. § 1915;

(3) denying a motion to dismiss under 8th Cir. R. 47A; and

(4) ordering a temporary stay of any proceeding pending the court's determination of a stay application.

(c) All Other Matters. A panel of three judges will act in all other matters.

(d) Reconsideration of Orders. Any party adversely affected by an order issued under subdivisions (a), (b), or (c) may file a motion to reconsider, vacate, or modify the order within 14 days after its entry. The motion will be referred to a three-judge panel that includes all judges who previously acted on the matter.

Cross-Reference: FRAP 27.

RULE 27B: FILING NOTICES OF APPEAL AND MOTIONS TO WITHDRAW IN CRIMINAL CASES

(a) Notices of Appeal. Retained counsel in criminal cases, and counsel appointed to represent a party pursuant to the provisions of the Criminal Justice Act, 18 U.S.C. § 3006A, Federal Rule of Criminal Procedure 44, or the inherent power of a federal court, shall file a notice of appeal upon their client's request. Defendant's trial counsel, whether retained or appointed, shall represent the defendant on appeal, unless the Court of Appeals grants permission to withdraw.

(b) Motions to Withdraw. A motion to withdraw on the ground that in counsel's opinion there are no non-frivolous issues to be urged on appeal must be accompanied by a brief prepared in accordance with the procedures enunciated in Anders v. California, 386 U.S. 738 (1967), and Robinson v. Black, 812 F.2d 1084 (8th Cir. 1987). A motion to withdraw on any other ground will only be granted for good cause shown, and will rarely be granted unless another attorney has entered an appearance for the defendant on appeal or another attorney has agreed to represent the defendant on appeal and the defendant has consented to the appearance of that new attorney.

RULE 28A: BRIEFS

(a) Briefs Filed by Registered CM/ECF Users. Briefs filed by attorneys and other registered CM/ECF users must be submitted for filing using the CM/ECF system by the date set forth in the court's briefing schedule. Upon receipt of the brief, the clerk will review the brief and determine whether it complies with the applicable Federal Rules of Appellate Procedure and Eighth Circuit Local Rules. If the brief complies with the rules, the clerk will file it and will send all parties a notice that the brief has been filed; registered CM/ECF users will receive their notice through an electronic Notice of Docket Activity, while attorneys and litigants who are not registered users will receive their notice by mail.

Attorneys exempt from CM/ECF use must submit their briefs through email to an account which the clerk's office will provide them. The clerk's office will follow the procedures set out in these rules for reviewing and filing these briefs. Upon receipt of notice that the electronic version of the brief has been accepted for filing, the attorney must comply with the other procedures concerning service and submitting the required number of paper copies.

(b) Correction of Defects and Effect of Failure to Comply with this Rule. If the brief does not comply with the rules, the clerk will notify the filer that the brief is defective and will allow the filer 5 days to submit a brief which complies with the rules. In the event an appellant fails to submit a revised opening brief that complies with the rules, the clerk will issue an order directing the filer to show cause why the appeal should not be dismissed for failure to prosecute. In the event any other filer, including an appellant filing a reply brief, fails to electronically submit a revised brief that complies with the rules, the clerk will enter an order directing the filer to show cause why an order should not be entered barring the filer from filing that brief.

(c) Briefs filed by Pro Se Litigants. Pro se litigants shall submit 1 paper copy of their merits briefs by the date set forth in the court's briefing schedule. No additional paper copies are required. The clerk will review the brief for compliance with the rules. If the brief is accepted for filing, the clerk will file the brief, scan it into the CM/ECF system and attach it to the docket. The clerk will then serve a Notice of Docket Activity on the registered users of CM/ECF showing that the brief has been filed. This electronic notice will constitute service of the brief on these parties. The clerk will notify the pro se litigant that the brief has been accepted for filing by sending the litigant a paper notice by mail.

(d) Paper Copies of Briefs for the Court and Parties. Registered CM/ECF users and exempt attorneys should not submit paper copies of the brief until the clerk has notified them that the brief has been reviewed and filed. Within 5 days of receipt of the notice that the brief has been filed, registered users and exempt attorneys must transmit 10 paper copies of the brief to the clerk of the court. Paper copies may be hand-delivered to the clerk's office in St. Louis or dispatched to the clerk's office in St. Louis in compliance with the provisions of FRAP 25(a)(2)(B). Within 5 days of receipt of the notice that the brief has been filed, attorneys must serve 1 copy of the paper brief on each party separately represented or proceeding pro se. Failure to submit paper copies will result in the issuance of an order to show cause.

(e) Additional Copies of Briefs in En Banc Cases. Eleven additional paper copies of briefs must be filed in cases heard en banc.

(f) Legibility. The clerk is authorized to reject pro se briefs on the ground that they are illegible and cannot be scanned. If a brief is rejected on this basis, the clerk shall notify the pro se party and allow a period of time for submission of a legible brief.

(g) Addendum to the Brief.

> (1) CONTENTS. Appellant must prepare an addendum and file it with the opening brief. The addendum must include:
>
>> (i) a copy of the district court or administrative agency opinion or order including supporting memoranda or findings; in an immigration case, the addendum should include both the IJ decision and the BIA decision; in a Social Security case, the addendum should include the ALJ decision, the Appeals Council decision and the district court's opinion; in a direct criminal appeal, the addendum should include the judgment and commitment order, as well as any other order, such as a suppression order, which forms the basis for an issue on appeal;
>>
>> (ii) any magistrate's report and recommendation that preceded the district court opinion or order;
>>
>> (iii) other relevant rulings of the district court.
>>
>> The addendum may also include up to 15 pages of excerpts from

the record that would be helpful in reading the brief without immediate reference to the appendix; examples of such materials include jury instructions at issue in the case, provisions of contracts or other key documents, and brief excerpts from the transcript.

(2) LENGTH. The addendum must not exceed 15 pages excluding the district court or agency opinion and orders and the magistrate's report and recommendation.

(3) APPELLEE'S ADDENDUM. The appellee's brief may include an addendum not to exceed 15 pages. Appellee's addendum must not duplicate materials contained in appellant's addendum.

(4) PAPER VERSION OF THE ADDENDUM. The addendum will normally be incorporated into the back of the paper version of the brief, but it may be bound separately if it includes a long district court opinion or report and recommendation. If bound separately, the appellant must file the same number of addenda as briefs.

(5) ELECTRONIC VERSION OF THE ADDENDUM. An electronic version of the addendum is required for every appellant's brief that is submitted electronically. An electronic version of the addendum is required for every appellee's brief submitted electronically if the appellee has elected to file the optional addendum provided for in Subsection (g)(3) of this rule. The CM/ECF system provides separate filing events for the submission of the brief and the addendum, and the electronic version of the addendum must be filed as a separate document and should not be attached to the electronic version of the brief. If the filer has access to digital version of the documents in the addendum, the documents should be converted to PDF files and submitted in PDF format. If the filer does not have access to digital versions of the documents, the addendum may be created by scanning paper copies of the documents and converting them to PDF images.

(h) Technical Requirements of the Electronic Version of the Brief.

(1) The electronic version of the brief submitted under Section (a) of this rule must be in a single document file.

(2) Counsel shall include a statement with the filing that the brief and

addendum have been scanned for viruses and that the brief is virus-free.

(3) The electronic version of the brief must be in Portable Document Format (also known as PDF or Acrobat Format). The electronic version of the brief must be generated by printing to PDF from the original word processing file, so that the text of the electronic version of the brief may be searched and copied.

(i) Contents of Briefs.

(1) SUMMARY OF THE CASE. Each appellant must file a statement not to exceed 1 page providing a summary of the case, the reasons why oral argument should or should not be heard, and the amount of time (15, 20, or 30 minutes, or in an extraordinary case, more than 30 minutes) necessary to present the argument. The summary must be placed as the first item in the brief. If appellee deems appellant's statement incorrect or incomplete, appellee may include a responsive statement in appellee's brief.

(2) STATEMENT OF ISSUES. In addition to the requirement of FRAP 28(a)(5), the statement of issues shall include for each issue a list of the most apposite cases, not to exceed 4, and the most apposite constitutional and statutory provisions.

(j) Incorporation by Reference. A party may not incorporate by reference the contents of a brief filed elsewhere.

(k) Motions to File Overlength Briefs. Motions for leave to file overlength briefs will be granted only in extraordinary cases. A motion for permission to file an overlength brief must be submitted at least 7 days prior to the brief's due date.

(l) Calculating Response Times. For registered users of CM/ECF, the time periods for filing appellee and reply briefs set out in FRAP 28.1, FRAP 29 and FRAP 31 shall be calculated from the date the court issues the Notice of Docket Activity filing the brief. The filing times for pro se parties and attorneys not registered for CM/ECF who receive their service by mail will be calculated in accordance with the provisions of FRAP 26(c).

Cross-References: FRAP 25 (filing and service), 26 (computation of time),

28, 29, 31, 32.

RULE 30A: DESIGNATED RECORD ON APPEAL

(a) Scope.

(1) SOCIAL SECURITY APPEALS.   Three copies of the administrative agency record must be filed in social security cases.

(2) PRO SE APPEALS. In all pro se appeals, the entire district court record is available for review. If the record is available in electronic format, the court will review the electronic version of the record. At the time a pro se notice of appeal is filed, the clerk of the district court must transmit to the clerk of this court the originals or paper copies of those portions of the original record which are not available through PACER, such as documentary exhibits, administrative records and state court files.

(b) Methods of Preparing the Record on Appeal.

(1) AGREED STATEMENT AS THE RECORD ON APPEAL. *See* FRAP 10(d).

(2) JOINT APPENDIX. *See* FRAP 30(a) & (b). Appellant must file 3 copies of the appendix with the brief.

(3) SEPARATE APPENDICES. Appellants may dispense with the process of preparing a joint appendix as set forth in FRAP 30(a) and (b) and submit a separate appendix with the opening brief. Appellant must notify the clerk and all opposing parties in writing of the decision to prepare and file a separate appendix within 14 days after filing the notice of appeal. Appellant must also order the transcript according to FRAP 10(b).

Appellees may file a separate appendix containing material not included in the appellant's appendix. Appellee must refer to record material found in appellant's separate appendix rather than duplicating the material.

Separate appendices must conform to FRAP 32(b) and must be fully indexed and consecutively paginated. Each party must file 3 copies of its separate appendix with its brief.

(4) SUPPLEMENTAL APPENDIX. If the parties conclude after the opening briefs have been filed that relevant material has been omitted from the joint appendix, they may agree to file a supplemental appendix. In the absence of agreement, either party may move this court to direct the clerk of the district court to transmit additional portions of the record.

In rendering judgment on appeal, this court may rely on any portion of the original record of the district court or the agency proceedings including portions not included in the designated record.

(c) Costs. The prevailing party may recover in this court the costs of reproducing the required number of copies of the appendix. Costs for producing the transcript may be recovered in the district court.

Unless the parties agree otherwise, the appellant must pay the cost of producing the joint appendix. The appellee, however, must advance to the appellant the cost of including parts of the record designated by appellee that the appellant deems unnecessary to determine the issues on appeal. If appellee prevails on appeal, the costs the appellee has advanced are recoverable. The cost of appellee's separate appendix is also recoverable.

The court will deny costs to parties who have caused unnecessary material to be inserted into the record. Any attorney who multiplies the proceedings in a case unreasonably and vexatiously may be held personally responsible by the court for excess costs according to 28 U.S.C. § 1927 and may be subject to disciplinary sanctions.

_____

Cross-References: FRAP 10, 11, 25 (filing and service), 26 (computation of time), 28, 30, 32; 8th Cir. R. 11A; 28 U.S.C. § 1927.

_____

RULE 32A: BRIEFS AND REPLY BRIEFS RESPONDING TO MULTIPLE BRIEFS

(a) Appellee Briefs in Consolidated Criminal Cases Involving Multiple Appellants. In consolidated criminal appeals involving multiple appellants, the United States must file a single appellee brief. The type-volume limitations set forth in FRAP 32(a)(7)(I) apply to the brief. If the United States believes presentation of the cases would be aided by separate appellee briefs, it may file a motion, at least 7 days prior to the brief due date, setting forth good cause to file separate briefs. Inability to comply with the type-volume limitations set forth in FRAP 32(a)(7)(B)(i) is not good cause for filing separate briefs.

(b) Appellee Briefs in Consolidated Civil Cases Involving Multiple Appellants. In consolidated civil cases involving multiple appellants, each separately-represented appellee must file a single appellee brief. The type-volume limitations set forth in FRAP 32(a)(7)(I) apply to the appellee brief.
(c) Reply Briefs in Appeals Involving Multiple Appellees. In cases involving multiple appellee briefs, appellant must file a single reply brief responding to all of the appellee briefs. The type-volume limitations set forth in FRAP 32(a)(7)(B)(ii) apply to the reply brief.

Rule 32.1A: CITATION OF UNPUBLISHED OPINIONS

Unpublished opinions are decisions which a court designates for unpublished status. They are not precedent. Unpublished opinions issued on or after January 1, 2007, may be cited in accordance with FRAP 32.1. Unpublished opinions issued before January 1, 2007, generally should not be cited. When relevant to establishing the doctrines of res judicata, collateral estoppel, or the law of the case, however, the parties may cite an unpublished opinion. Parties may also cite an unpublished opinion of this court if the opinion has persuasive value on a material issue and no published opinion of this court or another court would serve as well. A party citing an unpublished opinion in a document or for the first time at oral argument which is not available in a publically accessible electronic database must attach a copy thereof to the document or to the supplemental authority letter required by FRAP 28(j). When citing an unpublished opinion, a party must indicate the opinion's unpublished status.

RULE 33A: PREHEARING CONFERENCE PROGRAM

(a) Scope of Program. In any civil appeal included in the court's prehearing conference program, a conference will be held promptly to review, limit, or clarify the issues on appeal, to discuss settlement, and to consider any other matter relating to the appeal. This program does not apply to: petitions for postconviction relief, social security cases; cases dismissed below for lack of jurisdiction; interlocutory appeals certified under 28 U.S.C. § 1292(b); cases appealed under 28 U.S.C. § 1292(a)(1) and federal income tax cases.

(b) Proceedings. The conference will be conducted by the director of the prehearing conference program, or by a senior district judge on special assignment from the chief judge, at a site convenient to the parties. Conferences usually will be held in St. Louis, Missouri; St. Paul, Minnesota; or Little Rock, Arkansas.

(c) Confidentiality. Settlement-related material and settlement negotiations must be maintained in confidence by the director of the prehearing conference program or the senior district judge who conducts the conference. A judge who considers the appeal on its merits does not have access to settlement material, except as agreed by the parties.

Cross-Reference: FRAP 33.

RULE 34A: SCREENING FOR ORAL ARGUMENT

(a) Assignment of Screening Function. The chief judge may appoint the clerk, the senior staff attorney, or a panel or panels of judges of the court to screen cases awaiting disposition.

(b) Screening Categories. Cases may be screened for disposition without oral argument, for abbreviated argument, or for full argument. Cases screened for full oral argument usually will be allotted 10, 15 or 20 minutes per side. Extended argument of 30 minutes or more per side occasionally will be allotted.

(c) Reclassification by Hearing Panel. The panel assigned to dispose of a case may alter time allocations for oral argument or reclassify the case as suitable for disposition without oral argument.

(d) Disposition Without Oral Argument. The clerk will notify the parties when a case has been classified as suitable for disposition without argument. Any party may ask the court to reconsider the case for oral argument by filing a written request for reclassification within seven days after receiving notice.

(e) Calendar Designation. The clerk will indicate on the calendar the time allocated for argument of each case.

Cross-Reference: FRAP 34.

RULE 34B: ARGUMENT CALENDAR

Companion Cases. By order of the court, cases raising similar questions may be heard together. Counsel must inform the court if they know of pending cases that raise similar questions.

Cross-References: FRAP 34, 45(b).

RULE 35A: HEARING AND REHEARING EN BANC

Petition for En Banc Disposition. A petition must not refer to or adopt by reference any matter from other briefs or motions in the case.

> (1) NUMBER. Petitions for rehearing and rehearing en banc filed by attorneys and other registered CM/ECF users must be filed electronically through the CM/ECF system. Attorneys exempt from CM/ECF and pro se parties not participating in CM/ECF filing shall file one paper copy of the petition.

> (2) FRIVOLOUS PETITIONS; COSTS ASSESSED. The court may assess costs against counsel who files a frivolous petition for rehearing en banc deemed to have multiplied the proceedings in the case and to have increased costs unreasonably and vexatiously. At the court's order, counsel personally may be required to pay those costs to the opposing party. *See* 28 U.S.C. § 1927.

Cross-References: FRAP 35; 8th Cir. R. 4OA(b).

RULE 39A: TAXATION OF COSTS

(a) Taxation of Reproduction Costs. The cost of printing or otherwise reproducing necessary copies of briefs, separate addenda, and appendices must be taxable as follows:

(1) BRIEFS. Unless the court has directed the parties to file a greater number of briefs, the clerk will allow taxation of costs for only 10 copies of each brief, plus 1 copy for each party separately represented.

(2) SEPARATE ADDENDA. Unless the court has directed the parties to file a greater number of separate addenda, the clerk will allow taxation of costs for only 10 copies of each separate addendum prepared under 8th Cir. R. 28A(b)(2), plus 1 copy for each party separately represented.

(3) APPENDICES. Unless the court has directed the parties to file a greater number of appendices, the clerk will allow taxation of costs for only 3 copies of each appendix, plus 1 copy for each party separately represented.

(4) REPRODUCTION COSTS. The clerk will tax reproduction costs, regardless of reproduction method, at the following rate:

Reproduction per page per copy . . . . $ .15

Binding per brief, separate addendum, or appendix $2.00

Cover per brief, separate addendum, or appendix $2.00

Sales tax (if any) . . . . at the applicable rate

(5) OTHER COSTS. The clerk will not allow taxation of other costs associated with preparation of the brief or appendix. Parties cannot recover costs for overnight or special delivery.

(b) Filing Date. The prevailing party may file a bill of costs within 14 days after the entry of judgment. Untimely bills will be denied unless a motion showing good cause is filed with the bill. The losing party must file any objections to the bill of costs within 7 days after being served. If a party files a motion showing good cause, the clerk may grant a 7 day extension for filing either the bill of costs or the objections.

(c) Support for Bill of Costs. The bill of costs must be itemized and verified. Any receipts must be attached as exhibits to the bill of costs.

_____

Cross-References: FRAP 39(c), (d).
_____

RULE 40A: PETITION FOR REHEARING BY PANEL

(a) Number. Any party allowed to file pleadings in paper format must submit an original petition for rehearing; no copies are required.

(b) Treated as Petition for Rehearing En Banc. On the request of any judge on the panel, a petition for rehearing by a panel will be treated as a petition for rehearing en banc. Every petition for rehearing en banc, however, will automatically be deemed to include a petition for rehearing by the panel.

(c) Successive Petitions. Successive petitions for rehearing are not allowed. The clerk will accept for filing only 1 petition for rehearing from any party to an appeal and will not accept any motion to reconsider the court's ruling on a petition for rehearing or rehearing en banc.

_____

Cross-References: FRAP 27, 32(b), 35, 40; 8th Cir. R. 27A.
_____

RULE 42A: VOLUNTARY DISMISSAL OF CRIMINAL APPEALS

A criminal appeal may be dismissed only with the consent of the defendant. No motion to voluntarily dismiss a criminal appeal will be granted unless the defendant either signs the motion or consents, in a written attachment to the motion, to dismissal of the appeal.

RULE 45A: CLERK

Clerk to Furnish Copies. When an opinion is filed, the clerk will mail a copy to counsel for each of the parties. Additional copies of an opinion will be available from the clerk for $5.00 each.

Cross-Reference: FRAP 45.

RULE 46A: ADMITTING, SUSPENDING, AND DISCIPLINING ATTORNEYS

Applicants for admission must pay an admission fee of $190.00, for deposit in the Attorney Admission Fee Fund. An attorney who is appointed to represent a party proceeding in forma pauperis may appear in the case without being admitted to the bar of this court.

Cross-References: FRAP 46; 8th Cir. R. 47H.

RULE 46B: STUDENT PRACTICE

Any law student acting under a supervising attorney may appear and participate in proceedings in this court.

(a) Eligibility. To be eligible to appear and participate, a law student must:

> (1) be a student in good standing in a law school approved by the American Bar Association;

> (2) have completed legal studies equivalent to 3 semesters;

> (3) file with the clerk of court:

>> (I) a certificate from the dean of the law school or a faculty member

stating the student is of good moral character, satisfies the requirements listed above, and is qualified to serve as a legal intern;

(ii) a certificate stating the student has read and agrees to abide by the rules of the court, all applicable codes of professional responsibility, and other relevant federal practice rules;

(iii) a notice of appearance prescribed by the court and signed by the supervising attorney and the client in each case in which the student is participating or appearing as a law student intern; and

(4) be introduced to the court by an attorney admitted to practice in this court.

(b) Restrictions. No law student admitted under these rules may:

(1) request or receive compensation from the client;

(2) appear in court without the supervising attorney; or

(3) file any documents or papers with the court that have not been read, approved, and signed by the supervising attorney and cosigned by the student.

This restriction does not prevent the supervising attorney, law school, public defender, or government from paying compensation to the law student, or an agency from charging for its services.

(c) Supervising Attorneys. A person acting as a supervising attorney under this rule must be admitted to practice in this court and must:

(1) assume responsibility for the conduct of the student;

(2) read and sign pleadings, papers, and documents prepared by the student;

(3) advise the court of the student's participation, be present with the student at all times in court, and be prepared to supplement the student's oral or written work as the court requests or as necessary to ensure the client's proper representation; and

(4) be available to consult with the client.

(d) Special Notice of Appearance to be filed by law student:

SPECIAL NOTICE OF APPEARANCE

Supervising Attorney and Law Student

_____	_____
Title of Action	Case Docket No.

Please be advised that [name of supervising attorney] appears as attorney for [name of client] and is acting as supervising attorney for [name of law student], a law student who satisfies the requirements for student practice under 8 th Cir. R. 46B.

The supervising attorney and the law student have read and agree to abide by 8th Cir. R. 46B governing student practice.

_____		_____	
Supervising Attorney	Date	Law Student	Date
Address and Phone		Address and Phone	
_____		_____	
_____		_____	
		Law School Name and Address	
		_____	
		_____	
		_____	

Client Consent

I authorize [name of law student], who is being supervised by my attorney, [name of attorney], to appear in court and other proceedings on my behalf and to prepare documents on my behalf. My attorney must be present when the law student appears in court.

_____

Client   Date

Address

_____

_____

RULE 47A: SUMMARY DISPOSITION

(a) On Motion of Court. The court on its own motion may summarily dispose of any appeal without notice. However, in an in forma pauperis appeal in which a certificate of appealability has been issued, the court will afford 14 days' notice before entering summary disposition if the briefs have not been filed.

The court will dismiss the appeal if it is not within the court's jurisdiction or is frivolous and entirely without merit. The court may affirm or reverse when the questions presented do not require further consideration.

(b) On Motion of Parties. The appellee may file a motion to dismiss a docketed appeal on the ground the appeal is not within the court's jurisdiction. Except for good cause or on the motion of the court, a motion to dismiss based on jurisdiction must be filed within 14 days after the court has docketed the appeal.

On expiration of the time allowed for filing or express waiver of the right to file a response, or on receipt of the response, the clerk will distribute to the court the briefs filed, the record on appeal, and the motion and response. The court will consider the motion and enter an appropriate order.

Except as the court orders, the filing of a motion to dismiss does not toll the time limitations set forth in the Federal Rules of Appellate Procedure or these rules.

RULE 47B: AFFIRMANCE OR ENFORCEMENT WITHOUT OPINION

A judgment or order appealed may be affirmed or enforced without opinion if the court determines an opinion would have no precedential value and any of the following circumstances disposes of the matter submitted to the court for decision:

> (1) a judgment of the district court is based on findings of fact that are not clearly erroneous;

(2) the evidence in support of a jury verdict is not insufficient;

(3) the order of an administrative agency is supported by substantial evidence on the record as a whole; or

(4) no error of law appears.

The court in its discretion, with or without further explanation, may enter either of the following orders: "AFFIRMED. *See* 8th Cir. R. 47B"; or "ENFORCED. *See* 8th Cir. R. 47B."

RULE 47C: ATTORNEY FEES

(a) Motion for Fees. A motion for attorney fees, with proof of service, must be filed with the clerk within 14 days after the entry of judgment. The party against whom an award of fees is sought must file objections to an allowance of fees within 7 days after service. The court may grant on its own motion an allowance of reasonable attorney fees to a prevailing party.

(b) Determination of Fees. On the court's own motion or at the request of the prevailing party, a motion for attorney fees may be remanded to the district court or administrative agency for appropriate hearing and determination.

(c) Mandate. The clerk will prepare and certify an award of attorney fees granted by the court for insertion in the mandate. Issuance of a mandate will not be delayed for an award of attorney fees. If a mandate issues before final determination of a motion for attorney fees, the clerk of the district court, on the request of the clerk of this court, will add the award and its amendments to the mandate.

RULE 47D: ASSIGNMENT OF JUDGES; QUORUM

(a) Assignment of Judges; Quorum. According to 28 U.S.C. § 46, the judges of the court of appeals sit as the court directs. Unless a hearing or rehearing before the court en banc is ordered as provided by FRAP 35, a panel of not more than three judges will hear and determine all cases.

(b) Quorum; Absence of Quorum. A majority of the judges comprising the court constitutes a quorum. If less than a quorum is present on any day of the term, any judge in attendance may adjourn the court until a later time or, if no judge is present, the clerk may adjourn the court.

RULE 47E: DEATH OR DISABILITY OF JUDGE

If a judge sitting on a panel that has heard argument or taken under submission any appeal, petition, or motion becomes unable to consider the matter further because of death, illness, resignation, or incapacity, or is relieved of the case at the judge's request, the remaining 2 judges will determine the matter. Either remaining judge may, however, request the designation of a third judge. If either judge requests a designation or if the 2 judges do not agree on the matter, the chief judge will designate another circuit judge to sit in place of the judge who no longer serves on the panel. The clerk will advise the parties of a designation, but no further argument or additional briefs will be received unless the court orders otherwise.

RULE 47F: COURT LIBRARIES

The court's libraries are open to members of the Eighth Circuit bar, the United States Attorneys of the circuit and their assistants, other government law officers, and with permission, other public users. Only court personnel may remove books from the buildings where libraries are maintained.

RULE 47G: BAN ON PRACTICE OF LAW; POSTEMPLOYMENT RESTRICTION

No one employed as a staff attorney to the court, as a chambers attorney to a member of the court, or in any other capacity with the court, may engage in the practice of law while employed by the court. An employee must not participate in any way as an attorney in any case pending in the court during the employee's term of service, or appear at counsel table or on brief in any case for a period of one year after leaving court employment.

RULE 47H: ATTORNEY ADMISSION FEE FUND

(a) Use of Fund. The court will maintain an Attorney Admission Fee Fund to receive admission fees and other funds not required to be deposited in the Treasury of the United States. The fund may be used for:

(1) expenditures related to attorney admission proceedings;

(2) continuing legal education programs involving bench and bar;

(3) publication of rules, procedures, and plans of the court of appeals, the judicial council, or federal advisory committee for distribution to the bar;

(4) expenditures relating to the court's libraries;

(5) reimbursement of reasonable out-of-pocket expenses incurred by court-appointed attorneys representing indigents in civil cases not covered by the Criminal Justice Act; and

(6) any other purpose set out in the guidelines prepared by the Attorney Admission Fee Fund Committee and adopted by the court of appeals on July 2, 1985.

(b)   Custodian of Fund. The circuit executive will serve as custodian of the Attorney Admission Fee Fund. As custodian, the circuit executive will make expenditures from this fund as directed by the Attorney Admission Fee Fund Committee and the chief judge, will keep an account of the receipts and disbursements of the Fund for examination and approval by the Committee, and will give bonds as the Committee may require.

www.ingramcontent.com/pod-product-compliance
Lightning Source LLC
Chambersburg PA
CBHW080635290526
45790CB00007B/3071